"A" Is for Animals

by Annalisa McMorrow
illustrated by Marilynn G. Barr

Publisher: Roberta Suid
Design & Production: Standing Watch Productions
Cover Design: David Hale

Monday Morning Books
P.O. Box 1680
Palo Alto, CA 94302

E-mail us at: MMBooks@aol.com
Visit our Web site: www.mondaymorningbooks.com
Call us at: 1-800-255-6049

ISBN 1-57612-133-X

Printed in the United States of America
987654321

Contents

Introduction

A Is for Animals is a month-long unit that introduces children to the animal kingdom through informative and exciting cross-curriculum activities. Animal-related language, math, science, art, song, spelling, homework, and game activities are featured for each week.

This unit is divided into four weeks of activities. Each week is dedicated to a different type of animal habitat: deserts and plains, the polar regions, forests and mountains, and jungles and tropics.

Patterns throughout the unit can serve many purposes. For instance, duplicate the Portfolio Patterns for use as name tags, or desk labels, or enlarge them to use as bulletin board decorations. Patterns from the spelling activities also make useful bulletin board decorations. Simply white-out the spelling words and duplicate.

Share the information on "Animal Facts" with the children. Then help children make their Animal Portfolios. They can use these to share their assignments with their parents or to store all of their animal-related material in the classroom.

The activities in *A Is for Animals* are intended for grades one through three. Some lessons may easily be simplified for younger children. For instance, if children cannot write their own reports or stories, they can dictate them to the teacher or teacher's helper.

Throughout the unit, "Did You Know..." facts are listed in boxes on the teacher resource pages. Share these facts with the children, then have them look for facts on their own to share with their classmates.

Each week of the unit features a song or songs to be sung to familiar tunes. Consider holding a concert of all the songs at the end of the unit. Children might even want to try to write their own new songs to familiar tunes.

The unit ends with an Animal Diploma (p. 64). After completing all of the activities in the unit, give each of the students a diploma to show that they have mastered the world of animals.

To extend the *A Is for Animals* unit, look for animal-related books to store in your reading corner. (Several activities include book links about featured animals.) Children can spend free time learning more about the animals they're studying. Note that some books have an easy tie-in, such as the lion in *The Lion, the Witch, and the Wardrobe* or the elephants in *Babar*. Others are less obvious, such as the pet dog in *Tales of a Fourth Grade Nothing*. Challenge children to be on the lookout for mentions of animals in the books and magazines that they read on their own.

Also be on the lookout for games, puzzles, and toys with an animal theme. Some popular books, such as *Stellaluna*, have game and puppet tie-ins.

If possible, take the children on a field trip to a zoo or wildlife park to witness live animals in action. Or invite a veterinarian, zoologist, or pet store owner to visit the classroom and discuss animals.

The Web is a good place to locate information about animals to share with the students. Older children may be able to surf the Web themselves. Younger children may need assistance. Several Web sites are listed below as a starting point. Remember, Web sites change with frequency. Always check the sites yourself before sharing them with the students.

Animal Web Sites:

Chimpanzee Web Site
http://www.bev.net/education/SeaWorld/animal_bytes/chimpanzeeab.html

Elephant Web Sites
http://www.memo.com/zoo/exhibits/elephant.html
http://www.birminghamzoo.com/ao/mammal/afreleph.htm

Seal Web Site
http://www.clemetzoo.com/tourtrek2.html#seal

Tiger Web Sites
http://www.hdw-inc.com/HistoryCultureofWildCats.HTM
http://www.clemetzoo.com/tourtrek2.htm#tiger

Animal Facts

The animals featured in this book live in a wide variety of habitats. Here are facts about different animals to share with your class. Students may want to learn more about these animals (or others in this book). Help them to research animals on the Web!

There are two types of elephants. African elephants live in tropical Africa. Indian elephants are found in Southeast Asia. The African elephant is the largest living land mammal! It grows to 11 ft. (3.5 m) tall and weighs up to 8 tons (7,200 kg). Elephants use their trunks to grab food. They also drink water with their trunks.

Giraffes live in Africa. They eat green leaves from trees. They can spend 20 hours a day eating! A giraffe eats by pulling the leaves toward it with its sticky tongue. Giraffes can grow to be 18 ft. (6 m) tall. They can weigh more than 3,000 lbs (1,350 kg). Their coats are yellow with dark brown spots. Camouflaging helps them to blend in.

Llamas live in South America. They eat grassy reeds, mosses, lichens, and low shrubs. Llamas are related to camels. They are used to transport goods in areas where other types of transportation (such as cars) cannot go. Their wool is also used to make sweaters and blankets. Just like camels, llamas can go for days without water and with little food.

China is the home to pandas. A full-grown panda can be 6 ft. (1.8 m). Pandas mostly eat bamboo. Baby pandas are tiny. They weigh about as much as an apple. Although pandas look like bears, they are actually related to raccoons.

Animal Portfolio

Materials:
Portfolio Patterns (p. 8), scissors, crayons or markers, glue, hole punch, yarn, legal-sized folders or large sheets of heavy construction paper, stapler or tape (optional)

Preparation:
Duplicate a copy of the Portfolio Patterns for each child.

Directions:
1. Portfolios can be made in a variety of ways. Demonstrate at least one way for the children. If using legal-sized folders, punch holes along the two open sides. Cut two arm-length pieces of yarn and tie knots in one end of each. Thread the yarn through the holes and tie the free ends together to make a strap. If using construction paper, fold the paper in half to make a folder, and then continue as described above. If making portfolios as shown in the picture, punch two holes on opposite sides, thread through with a piece of yarn, and tie. Consider sealing the sides with tape or staples.
2. Give each child a sheet of patterns to color and cut out.
3. Have the children decorate their portfolios with the patterns.

Options:
• The children can add their own hand-drawn pictures. Or they can cut out magazine pictures to glue to their portfolios.
• Cover the portfolios with contact paper for added sturdiness. Strengthen the holes with reinforcers.

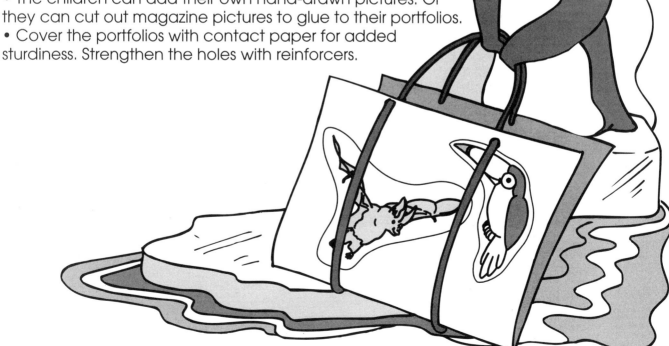

Portfolio Patterns

A Is for Animals © 2001 Monday Morning Books

If I Were a . . .

The Harry Potter series is the perfect tie-in for this activity. However, it can be completed without the books, as well.

Materials:
My Animal Graphic Organizer (p. 10), paper, pens or pencils, crayons or markers, encyclopedias and animal-related resources, Harry Potter book (optional)

Preparation:
1. Duplicate a copy of the graphic organizer for each child.
2. Gather encyclopedias and other animal-related nonfiction resources for the children to use.

Directions:
1. Read the opening chapter of *Harry Potter and the Sorcerer's Stone* by J.K. Rowling (Scholastic, 1997). In it, one of the characters transforms herself into a cat.
2. Have each child choose an animal that he or she would like to be able to turn into. This animal should live in the plains region, such as antelopes, cheetahs, elephants, gazelles, giraffes, lions, or zebras.
3. Have the children do research to learn three positive and three negative facts about their chosen animals. They should use their graphic organizers to help stay focused.
4. Have the children use the facts they learned to write short essays about why they would (or would not) like to be their chosen animals.

Option:
• If not reading a Harry Potter book, simply have the children choose an animal and write about why they would or would not like to be that animal.

My Animal Graphic Organizer

Name _____

Date _____

The animal I'm researching is:

_____

This animal lives in _____

These are the positive facts that I found:

1. _____

2. _____

3. _____

These are the negative facts that I found:

1. _____

2. _____

3. _____

How Many Stripes?

This zebra math activity can be used for different levels of mathematical study. For younger children, write a plus or minus sign between the striped zebras of each equation. Write in a multiplication sign for older children.

Materials:
Zebra Math (p. 12), pencils

Preparation:
1. Fill in the missing signs (+, -, or x), then duplicate the Zebra Math pages. Make one for each child.
2. Make an answer key for self-checking, if desired.

Directions:
1. Give each child a copy of the Zebra Math.
2. Have the children do the problems. They count the stripes on the first zebra and the second zebra, then see whether they are doing an addition, subtraction, or multiplication problem. They draw the correct number of stripes on the final zebra.
3. Children can share their answers with the class. Or they can use the answer key for self-checking.

Options:
• For older children, pass out the Zebra Math pages without any signs written in the middle grass. Let the children make their own problems to test their friends. They can add a +, -, or x and then write the answers on the back. Have the children trade papers.
• To make the problems more difficult, add more stripes to the zebras.

Zebra Math

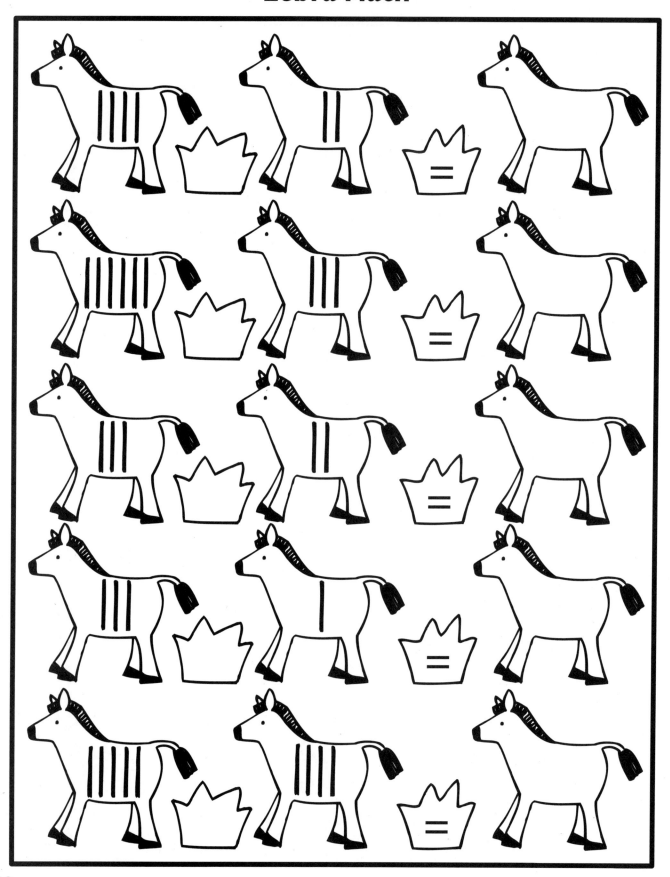

A Is for Animals © 2001 Monday Morning Books

Elephant Words

Materials:
Elephants (p. 14), scissors, tape, books about elephants or the "e" volume of the encyclopedia, pens or pencils, paper

Preparation:
1. Duplicate enough elephant patterns so that each child can have one.
2. Gather books about elephants.

Directions:
1. Give each child one elephant pattern to cut out.
2. Provide an assortment of elephant books for the children to look through to gather words that relate to elephants. They should write down 10 to 20 words. (These might be adjectives, such as "large" or "gray," or they might be nouns or proper nouns, such as "tusk," "trunk," or "Africa.")
3. Have the children put the elephants on sheets of paper. They should use the elephants as templates and write the words they chose around the templates. When they remove the elephant templates, there will be an elephant shape made by an outline of elephant-related words.
4. Post the completed pictures in a chain on a bulletin board or wall.

Note:
• Younger children can gather fewer words and use them to trace around the baby elephants.

Did You Know...
Elephants in Africa can sometimes live for 80 or 100 years.

large

gray

Africa

tusk

India

toes

ivory

trunk

ears

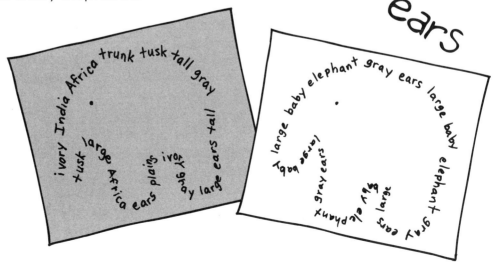

Elephants

A Is for Animals © 2001 Monday Morning Books

Spelling Safari

Materials:
Plains Animals (p. 16), Jeep (p. 17), bag, construction paper, scissors, colored markers

Preparation:
1. Duplicate a copy of the Plains Animals for each child and one for teacher use.
2. Cut the teacher's set of animals apart and color.
3. Enlarge the Jeep pattern, cut out and color, and post on a bulletin board.

Directions:
1. Announce a date for a spelling safari.
2. Give each child a copy of the animal patterns to color and cut apart. They should take the animals home to study.
3. Divide the students into small groups. Have the children work together to learn the words.
4. On the day of the spelling safari, put the animals in a bag. Pull one animal from the bag at a time and have a child from each group spell the word on the animal.
5. If the child spells the word correctly, he or she can post the animal in front of the jeep. If not, another child from that group tries to spell the word.
6. Continue until each child has a chance to spell one word, and all of the animals are posted on the board.

Options:
• If the words are too difficult, white-out the given spelling words and write in your own. Duplicate these for the class.
• Use the words on the list for a match-up activity. Have the children match the two words that are related. The answers are: elephant/tusk, giraffe/spots, lion/pride, zebra/stripe.
• Draw a picture of yourself in the jeep before posting it.

Plains Animals

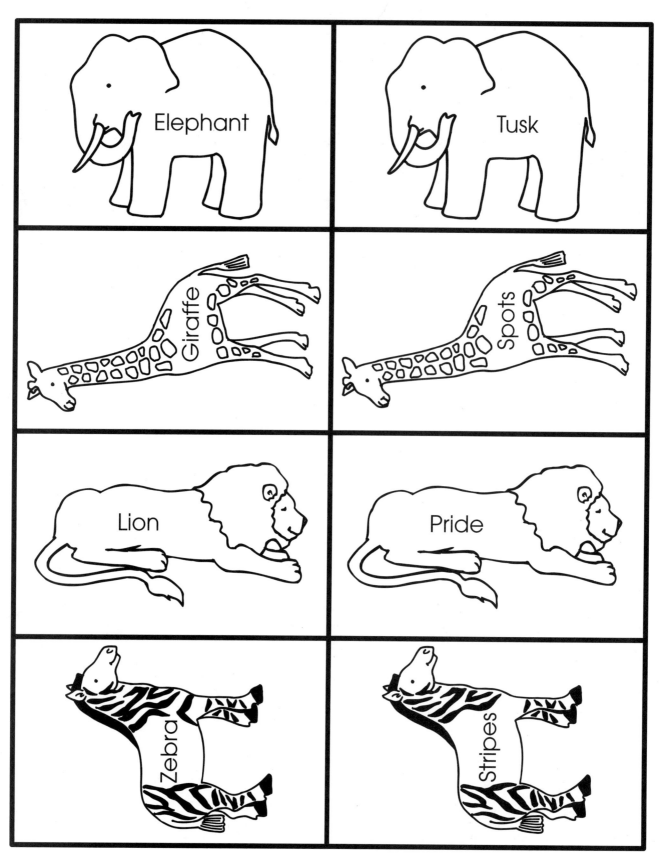

Elephant

Tusk

Giraffe

Spots

Lion

Pride

Zebra

Stripes

A Is for Animals © 2001 Monday Morning Books

Jeep

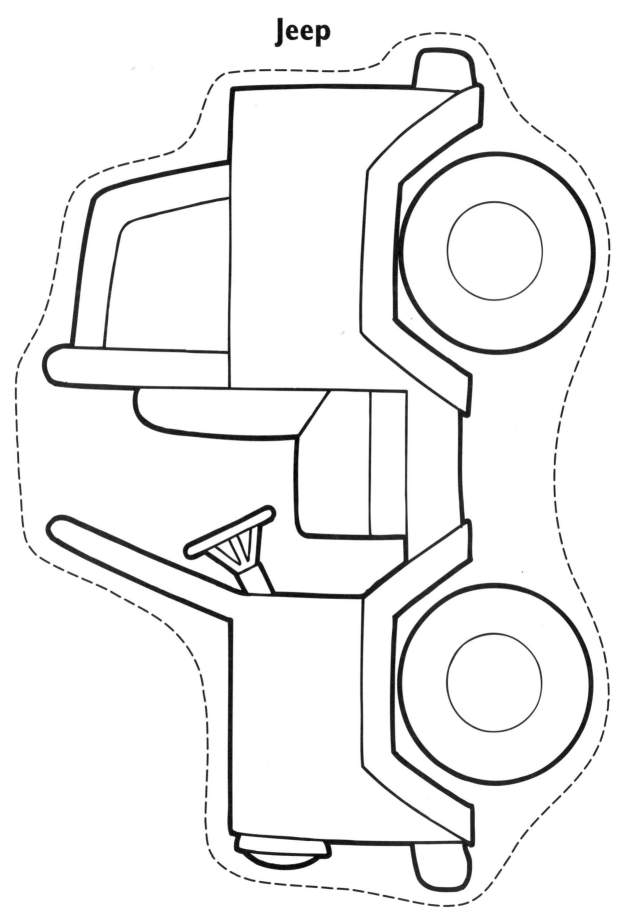

Fake Fur Books

Most scientists keep journals to record observations about experiments. Treat your students like real scientists and have them keep their own animal journals. They can draw pictures of animals that they see outside of the classroom in their books.

Materials:
Encyclopedias or animal-related nonfiction resources, colored construction paper, crayons or markers, drawing paper, scissors, hole punch, yarn or brads

Preparation:
None

Directions:
1. Explain that while some fashion designers use real animal skins for clothes, others use fake fur. The children will be making books with fake-animal print covers.
2. Have the children use encyclopedias or animal-related resources to learn about the body coverings of animals in the plains region.
3. Let the children choose colored construction paper to use for their book covers. Have them draw an animal-print design for the covers. They should choose an animal from the plains, such as a zebra or cheetah or giraffe.
4. Have the children cut white drawing paper to fit the book covers. They can add designs to the covers using crayons or markers.
5. Help the children bind their books with yarn or brads.
6. The children can use the books to keep track of animals they see during the unit.

Spots & Stripes

Materials:
Animal Match-Up Cards (p. 20), scissors, crayons or markers, envelopes (one per child)

Preparation:
1. Duplicate a copy of the Animal Match-Up Cards for each child.
2. Make one set for yourself. Glue the correct hides to the animals to make an answer key.

Directions:
1. Give each child a copy of the cards to color and cut apart.
2. Have the children try to match the hides to the animals.
3. The children can store the match-up cards in the envelopes. They can take the cards home to share with their families.

Option:
• Have the children learn one fact about each of the animals shown in the game.

Animal Match-Up Cards

A Is for Animals © 2001 Monday Morning Books

Animal Songs

Have You Ever Laughed
(to the tune of "Do Your Ears Hang Low?")

Have you ever laughed
    at the neck of a giraffe?
Have you seen giraffes eat leaves
    from the tippy-tops of trees?
A giraffe is very tall;
    it must think that we are small.
Have you ever laughed?

The Special Words
(to the tune of "Mocking Bird")

Did you know there are special words
For groups of animals, bugs, and birds?

There's a down of hares and a skein of geese,
and a rowdy troup of apes or chimpanzees.

Lots of lions are called a pride,
and a bunch of goats are called a tribe.

There's a gang of elk and a cloud of gnats,
A clutch of chicks and a clouder of cats.

A head is a bunch of elephants,
And a colony's the name for a group of ants.

There's a gam of whales, yes, that's the rule,
And a lot of fish are in a school.

Many giraffes make up a herd,
And those are some animal naming words.

A Pride of Alley Cats

Materials:
Paper, markers, pencils

Preparation:
1. Create a tally sheet of animals that live in your area. Choose animals that the children might see around their neighborhoods. Depending on your region, these might include cats, dogs, squirrels, cows, pigs, deer, or kangaroos.
2. Duplicate a copy for each child.

Directions:
1. Discuss the fact that groups of animals have different names. For example, a group of lions is called a pride and a group of zebras is called a herd.
2. Give each child a tally sheet and have the children mark how many of each animal they see during a weekend. (Remind the children not to disturb the animals.)
3. Have the children bring their tally sheets back to share with the class.
4. Total the number of different animals that the children saw, ranking the number from greatest to least. Then have the children give names to the groups of animals. They can use the names given to plains animals.

Group Animal Names:
head of elephants
pride of lions
herd of zebra or giraffes

Did You Know...
Lions live in prides of up to 30. Zebras live in herds of up to 1,000.

A Is for Animals © 2001 Monday Morning Books

Rain Forest Trading Cards

Children will create trading cards of rain forest creatures with illustrations and facts.

Materials:
Rain Forest Trading Cards (p. 24), rain forest resources, paper, pens or pencils, crayons or markers, scissors

Preparation:
1. Duplicate a copy of the cards for each child.
2. Gather rain forest-related books for children to use.

Directions:
1. Give each child a copy of the cards. The children can cut them apart and color them as desired.
2. Explain that the children will be making their own trading cards. Have the children choose a rain forest animal to research. (Refer to the list below.)
3. Have the children use books to find pictures of their animals. They might also use the Web.
4. The children should draw pictures of their animals. Then the children can trade cards, if they want to.

Options:
• Younger children can use the Rain Forest Trading Cards to play a game of concentration. Duplicate two copies of the cards for each game.
• Older children can add facts about the animals or the rain forest to their pictures.

Rain Forest Animals (and insects):
Army ants, ape, anteater, armadillo, bat, boa constrictor, centipede, chimpanzee, coral snake, eagle, fruit bat, flying fox, gecko, gorilla, gypsy moth, hummingbird, howler monkey, jaguar, kinkajou, leaf-cutter ant, ocelot, orangutan, parrot, piranha, praying mantis, porcupine, Queen Alexandra birdwing butterfly, red fan parrot, sloth, slug, spider monkey, tarantula, tree frog, toucan, vampire bat, wasp, woolly monkey

Rain Forest Trading Cards

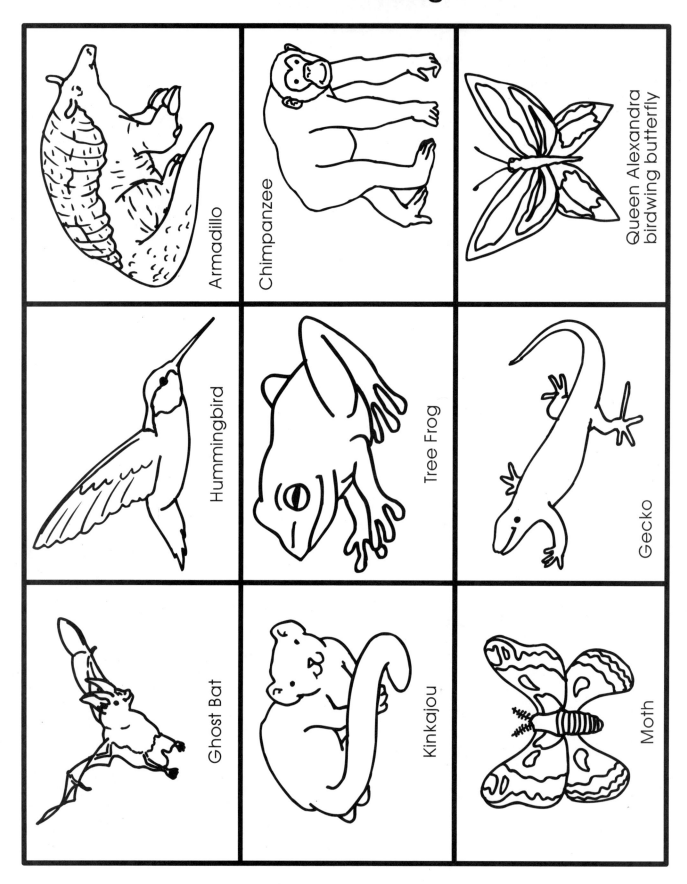

Counting Chimps

This chimpanzee math activity can be used for different levels of mathematical study. For younger children, write a plus or minus sign in the middle chimp of each equation. Write in a multiplication sign for older children.

Materials:
Chimpanzee Math (p. 26), pencils

Preparation:
1. Fill in the missing signs (+, -, or x), then duplicate the Chimpanzee Math page. Make one for each child.
2. Make an answer key for self-checking, if desired.

Directions:
1. Give each child a copy of the Chimpanzee Math.
2. Have the children do the problems. They see whether they are doing an addition, subtraction, or multiplication problem. Then they write the correct answer on the leaf.
3. Children can share their answers with the class. Or they can use the answer key for self-checking.

Option:
• For older children, pass out the Chimpanzee Math pages without any signs written in the chimps. Let the children make their own problems to test their friends. They can add a +, -, or x and then write the answers on the back. Check the children's work. Then have them trade papers.

> **Did You Know...**
> Although gorillas look scary, they are actually gentle creatures. They eat nuts, berries, and fruits.

Chimpanzee Math

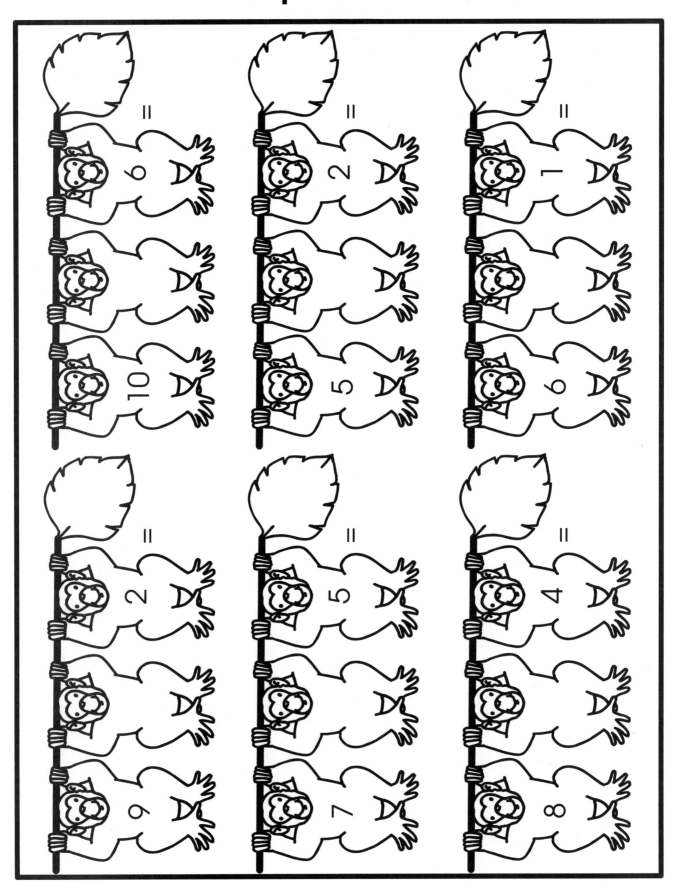

Cool Camouflage

Certain animals and insects use camouflage to blend in with their surroundings. They do this to hide from their enemies or to help them sneak up on their prey.

Materials:
Rain forest patterns from this chapter, books about rain forests, paper, crayons and markers

Preparation:
Duplicate copies of the rain forest animal patterns found in this chapter.

Directions:
1. Describe camouflage to the children. Ask if the children know of any animals or insects in your area that use camouflage, such as grasshoppers.
2. Have the children look at the patterns of the rain forest animals.
3. Show the children pictures of a rain forest, and have them draw their own rain forest backgrounds.
4. Have the children draw their own versions of the animals, or let the children use the animal patterns to glue to their pictures. They should color the animals to blend in with their backgrounds.

> **Did You Know...**
> An ocelot uses its spotted coat to blend in with the leaves of the trees.

Sloth Spelling

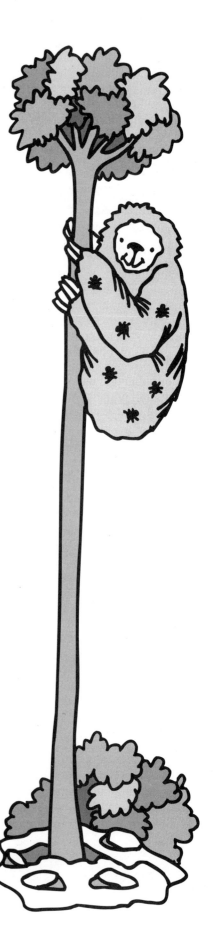

Sloths provide homes to a variety of animals! Beetles, mites, and moths can live in a sloth's fur. This activity uses the sloth as a background on which to post the spelling words.

Materials:
Bugs (p. 29), Sloth (p. 30), bag, construction paper, scissors, colored markers

Preparation:
1. Duplicate a copy of the Bugs for each child and one for teacher use.
2. Cut the bugs apart and color as desired.
3. Enlarge the Sloth pattern and post on a bulletin board.

Directions:
1. Announce a date for a spelling bee.
2. Divide the students into small groups. Have the children work together to learn the words. Let the children take the words home to study.
3. On the day of the spelling bee, put the bugs in a bag. Pull one bug from the bag at a time and have a child from each group spell the word on the bug.
4. If the child spells the word correctly, he or she can post the bug on the sloth. If not, another child from that group tries to spell the word.
5. Continue until each child has a chance to spell one word and all of the bugs are posted on the board.

Options:
• Duplicate extra copies of the blank bug and write in additional spelling words.
• If the words are too difficult, white-out the given spelling words and write in your own. Duplicate these for the class.

Did You Know...
One sloth was found with 978 beetles living in its fur! The word sloth comes from a word meaning slow. Sloths move extremely slowly.

Bugs

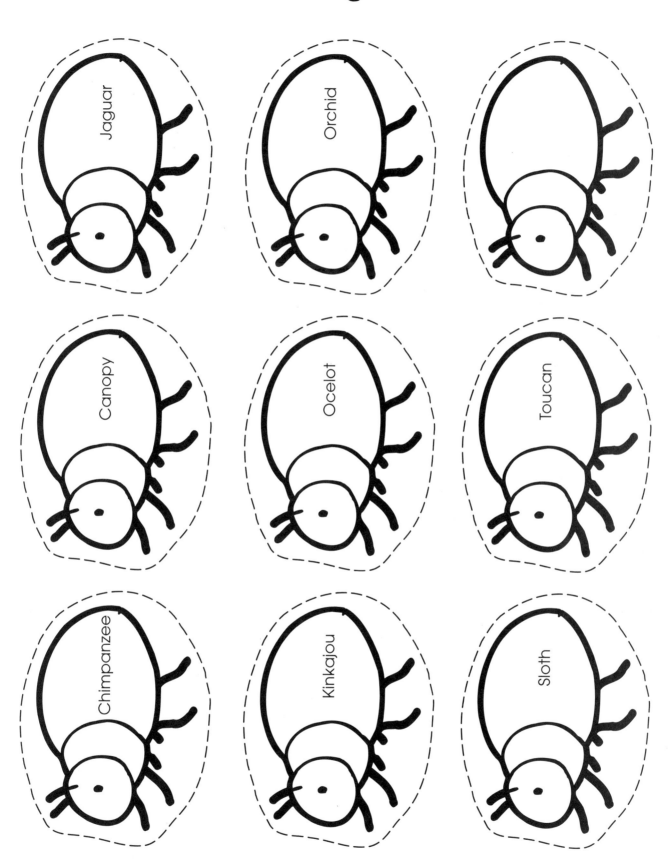

Jaguar

Orchid

Canopy

Ocelot

Toucan

Chimpanzee

Kinkajou

Sloth

Sloth

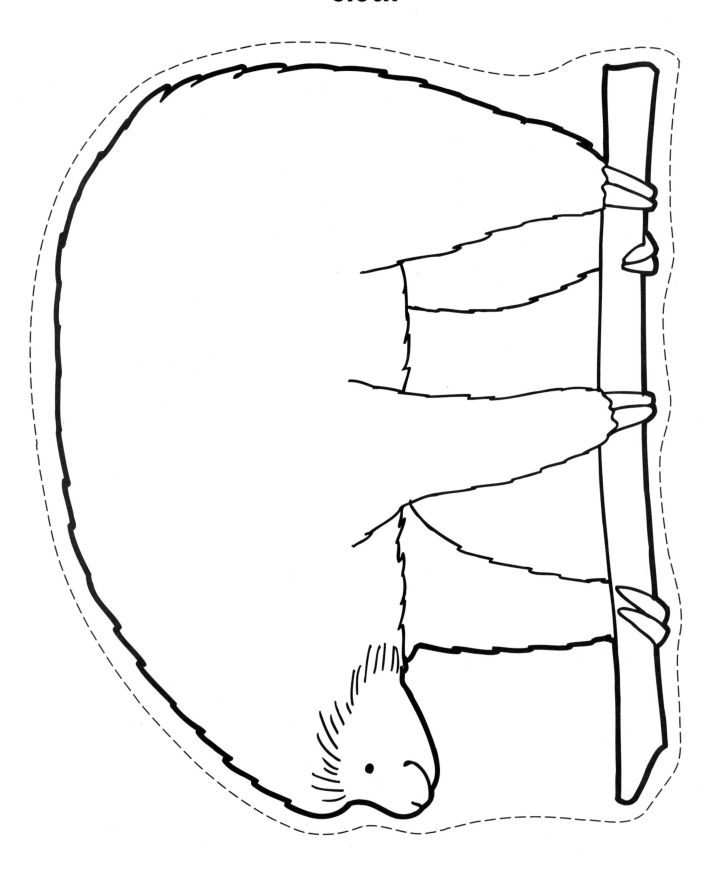

Cooperative Canopy

Children work together to paint a mural depicting a rain forest. Then they add pictures of rain forest animals to the mural.

Materials:
Rain Forest Animals (p. 32), large sheet of paper, tempera paints, paintbrushes, shallow tins (for paints), rain forest resources, scissors, glue

Preparation:
Duplicate and enlarge the Rain Forest Animals and cut them apart. Make enough for each child to have one animal to color.

Directions:
1. Explain that the children will be painting a mural to look like a rain forest.
2. Describe the layers of a rain forest: the lowest level is called the forest floor. Most nutrients are on top of the soil, so the trees have shallow roots. The understory is from near the ground to 40 or 50 ft. (12 to 15 m) in the air. The next layer is the canopy. It's made of trees that are usually 60 to 90 ft. (18 to 27 m) tall. The top layer is the emergent layer. It's made of the tops of the tallest trees in the rain forest. Different animals live on different levels.
3. Provide a variety of colored paints for the children to paint a rain forest mural.
4. Let the children choose rain forest animals to color then post in the appropriate levels. (The spider and snake are on the forest floor. The kinkajou, frog, and monkey are on the understory. The birds and butterfly can be in the canopy or the emergent layer.)
5. Hang the dry mural on a wall in the classroom.

Option:
• The children can draw their own animal patterns to glue to the picture.

> **Did You Know...**
> The tallest trees in the rain forest can be up to 200 ft. (60 m) tall!

Rain Forest Animals

A Is for Animals © 2001 Monday Morning Books

Jungle Jeopardy

This game is played a bit like the "Jeopardy" game on television. In this case, the children choose whether statements are true or false.

Materials:
Sneaky Statements (p. 34), scissors, index cards, pencils, resource books about rain forests and jungles

Preparation:
None

Directions:
1. Explain the game. You will read a statement. Children who think they know whether it is true or false will raise their hands. Choose one child to answer. If he or she is correct, let this child read the next statement. If not, read the next statement yourself.
2. Once the children understand the game, have each child create his or her own true/false statement. The children should write the statement on one side of an index card and the correct answer on the back. They can use information from this book or from resource books about rain forests and jungles.
3. Gather all of the children's statements and continue with the quiz game. Or let the children quiz each other.

Option:
• Create a point system where statements are given a certain number of points based on the level of difficulty. Have a final jeopardy run-off between the children with the most points.

Sneaky Statements

1. Different types of bugs live on a sloth.
True

2. A rain forest canopy is a type of hammock.
False

3. Gorillas are vegetarians.
True

4. A sloth moves extremely fast.
False

5. Jaguars are big, striped cats.
False

6. Ocelots use the spots on their coats to blend in with the leaves.
True

7. Different animals live on different levels of the rain forest.
True

8. Camouflage is the name for the top level of the rain forest.
False

Final Jeopardy Statement:
Tarantulas live in the forest canopy.
False. Tarantulas live on the forest floor!

A Is for Animals © 2001 Monday Morning Books

Jungle Jingles

Do You Have Some Spots
(to the tune of "You're a Grand Old Flag")

Do you have some spots,
Just a few or a lot,
Do you prowl through the jungle all day?
When you want a snack
Do you attack
By pouncing on top of your prey?

You can blend right in
With the rain forest din,
And take naps hidden by the leaves.
Because a jaguar sleeps wherever it wants,
And it likes hiding in the trees.

Oh, Give Me a Tree
(to the tune of "Home on the Range")

Oh, give me a tree,
Said the young chimpanzee,
I will swing from the branches all day,
I'll hide in the leaves,
With other chimpanzees,
For that is the rain forest way.

In forests today,
Fewer animals have space to play,
What needs to be heard
Are encouraging words.
Once they're gone,
We'll have nothing to say.

Rain Forest Reading

Children will use these bookmarks to keep track of the different rain forest-related materials that they read.

Materials:
Bookmarks (this page), crayons or markers, scissors

Preparation:
Duplicate enough copies of the bookmarks so that each child can have one.

Directions:
1. Have the children cut out and color the bookmarks.
2. Explain that each time the children read a book, they should write the title on the bookmark.
3. When the children finish the bookmark, they can make their own to continue to track their reading.

Options:
• Children can make bookmarks for friends or family members.
• Duplicate other patterns from this book for the children to use to make bookmarks.
• Make a large classroom chart to show the books that all of the children have read. Set a goal for how many books the class should read by a specific date.
• Have the children rate their favorite books on their bookmarks. They can give four stars for ones they really like, three for books they like, and so on.

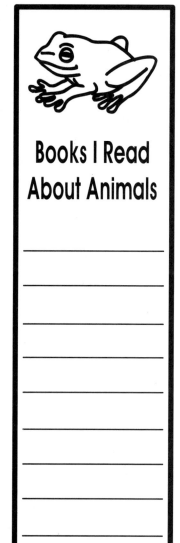

Books I Read About Animals

_____

_____

_____

_____

_____

_____

_____

_____

_____

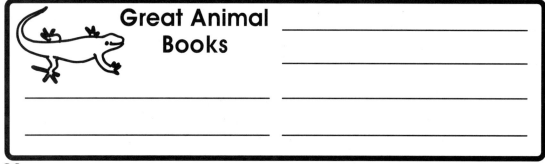

Great Animal Books

_____

_____

_____

_____

_____

_____

Mary Had a Polar Bear

Materials:
Mother Goose Rhymes (p. 38), paper, pens or pencils, books of Mother Goose or other children's rhymes

Preparation:
Duplicate a copy of the rhymes for each child.

Directions:
1. Read the rhymes with the students.
2. Explain that the children will be rewriting the rhymes and replacing the animals in the rhymes with animals that live in the Arctic. Work together as a class to rewrite one rhyme.
3. Let the children each choose rhymes to rewrite. They can choose from those on the sheet or from books of rhymes. Explain that it is easiest to simply replace words inside a rhyme—so that the rhyme itself stays the same. Children can experiment with different rhymes.
4. Hold a poetry reading in which the children recite their rewritten rhymes.

Options:
• Let the children work together in pairs or small groups.
• Provide rhyming dictionaries.
• Have children work to include facts in their rhymes.
• Create a book of student-written poetry.

Example:

Mary had a polar bear.
It blended with the snow.
And everywhere that Mary went,
That bear was sure to go.

It followed her to school one day,
Which was against the rule,
No polar bears allowed inside,
They need a place that's cool!

Mother Goose Rhymes

Little Miss Muffet
Little Miss Muffet sat on a tuffet
Eating her curds and whey.
Along came a spider and sat down beside her
And frightened Miss Muffet away.

Leg over Leg
Leg over leg as the dog went to Dover
It came to a stile, and up it went over!

The Man in the Moon
The man in the moon looked out of the moon,
And this is what he said.
"It's time now that I'm getting up,
All babies went to bed!"

Bye, Baby Bunting
Bye, Baby Bunting,
Daddy's gone a-hunting
To get a little rabbit skin,
To wrap a Baby Bunting in.

Twinkle, Twinkle, Little Star
Twinkle, twinkle, little star,
How I wonder what you are.
Up above the world so high,
Like a diamond in the sky.
Twinkle, twinkle, little star,
How I wonder what you are.

Baa, Baa, Black Sheep
Baa, Baa, Black Sheep,
Have you any wool?
Yes, sir, yes, sir,
Three bags full.
One for my master, one for my dame,
And one for the little boy who lives in the lane.

Placing Penguins

Art and math are combined in this fun, penguin-themed activity.

Materials:
Penguin Patterns (p. 45), large sheet of paper, tempera paint, paintbrushes, shallow tins (for paint), scissors, glue, crayons or markers

Preparation:
Duplicate enough copies of the penguins for each child to have several.

Directions:
1. Give the children the penguin patterns to cut out.
2. Have the children paint a backdrop for the penguins. They can draw a sea and ice floes.
3. The children should glue their penguins to the picture. They can add drawings of nests, eggs, and baby penguins, as well.
4. Once the picture has dried, use the mural as a basis for math problems. For instance, have the children count how many of the penguins are on the ice and how many are in the water. Then have them:
• subtract the smaller number from the larger
• add the numbers to get the total amount of penguins
• multiply the numbers
5. Once the children see how you are creating math problems, have each child make up one addition, subtraction, or multiplication problem that uses the penguins.

Did You Know...
Penguins nest in colonies of up to half a million birds in 500 acres.

Polar Bear Blending

Materials:
Polar Bear (p. 41), pens or pencils, books about polar
bears, large sheet of white paper, glue

Preparation:
1. Collect a variety of resources about polar bears.
2. Duplicate a copy of the Polar Bear for each child.

Directions:
1. Explain to the children that polar bears blend in with
their snowy surroundings. The bears have even been
known to hold one paw over their black noses when
hunting to further camouflage themselves.
2. Give each child a copy of the polar bears to cut out.
3. Have the children look for polar bear facts in the
resource books.
4. Explain that the children will be making a mural of polar
bears. They should use the resource books to find words
that describe polar bears.
5. Have the children glue or tape the patterns on the large
sheet of white paper, then write the words they've chosen
as outlines for the bears. It's all right for children to repeat
words.
6. Post the completed polar bear mural in the classroom.

Option:
• Glue the blank seals (p. 43) to the mural, as well.

A Is for Animals © 2001 Monday Morning Books

Polar Bear

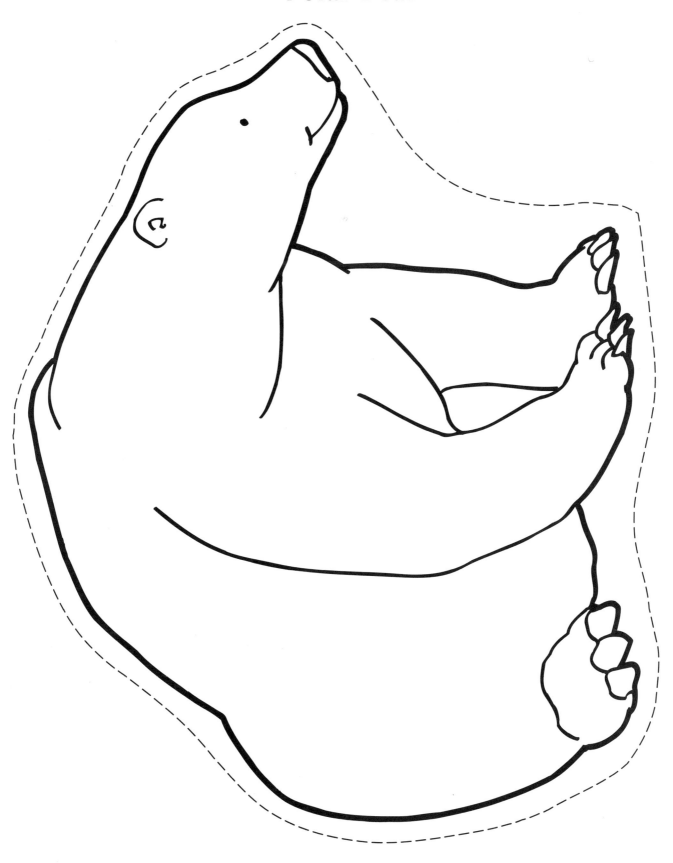

Super Seal Spelling

Seals are mammals with streamlined bodies. They can be found in a variety of regions, including both the Antarctic and warmer waters of the Mediterranean, Caribbean, and Hawaiian seas.

Materials:
Seals (p. 43), bag, dark and light blue construction paper, construction paper, scissors, colored markers

Preparation:
1. Duplicate a copy of the Seals for each child and one for teacher use.
2. Cut the seals apart and color as desired.
3. Create a sea background with the dark blue paper. Use the lighter blue as a piece of ice for the seals to perch on.

Directions:
1. Announce a date for a spelling bee.
2. Divide the students into small groups. Have the children work together to learn the words. Let the children take the words home to study.
3. On the day of the spelling bee, put the seals in a bag. Pull one seal from the bag at a time and have a child from each group spell the word on the seal.
4. If the child spells the word correctly, he or she can post the seal on the board, either in the water or on the ice. If not, another child from that group tries to spell the word.
5. Continue until each child has a chance to spell one word, and all of the seals are posted on the board.

Options:
• Write additional spelling words in the blank seals.
• If the words are too difficult, white-out the given spelling words and write in your own. Duplicate these for the class.

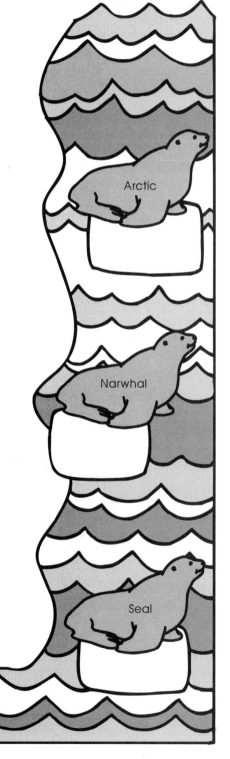

Seals

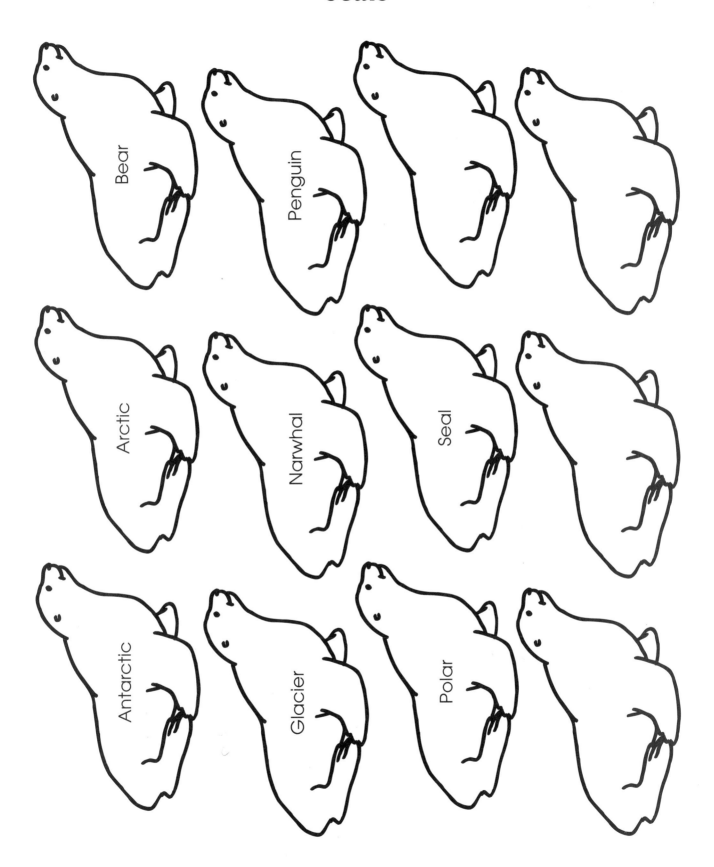

Bear

Penguin

Arctic

Narwhal

Seal

Antarctic

Glacier

Polar

Penguin Paper Dolls

Penguins look like they are wearing tuxedos. With this activity, the children can make other clothes for penguin paper dolls.

Materials:
Penguin Patterns (p. 45), Paper Clothes (p. 46), crayons or markers, scissors, heavy paper or cardstock, construction paper, art extras (sequins, glitter, glue), paper clips, envelopes (one per child)

Preparation:
Duplicate a copy of the penguins and clothes for each child. For longer lasting dolls, duplicate the penguins onto heavy paper or cardstock.

Directions:
1. Give the children the penguins and paper clothes to color and cut out.
2. The children can attach the clothes to the penguins using paper clips.
3. Let the children make their own clothes for the penguins from colored construction paper.
4. The children can store their penguins and clothes in the envelopes.

Did You Know...
Penguins live in the Antarctic. They swim using flipper-like wings and waddle when on land. The largest are the emperor penguins (3-4 ft./91.5-122 cm tall).

Penguin Patterns

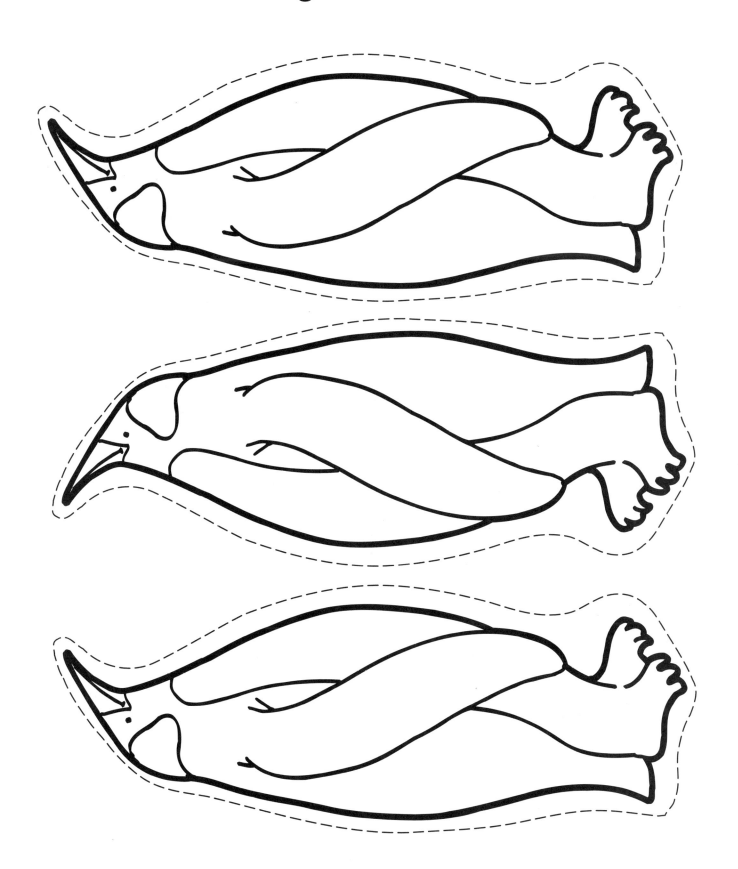

Paper Clothes

Who Wants to Be a Zoologist?

Zoology is the study of animals. Children will challenge each other with multiple-choice questions to share what they know about the animals they've studied throughout this unit.

Materials:
Quiz Questions (p. 48), scissors, index cards, pencils, resource books about animals

Preparation:
None

Directions:
1. Explain the game. You will read off a question and four possible answers. Children who think they know the answer will raise their hands. Choose one to answer. If he or she is correct, let this child read the next question. If not, keep going until a child answers correctly.
2. Once the children understand the game, have each child create his or her own question with four possible answers. The children should write the question and answers on one side of an index card and the correct answer on the back. They can use information from this book or from resource books about animals. Be sure to explain that three of the answers should be incorrect and only one will be correct.
3. Gather all of the children's questions and continue with the quiz game. Or let the children quiz each other.

Options:
• Let the children have a chance to remove two incorrect answers.
• Allow children to confer with a friend about the correct answer.

Did You Know...
Narwhals' tusks were once sold as "unicorn horns." Narwhals use their horns for jousting.

Quiz Questions

1. How does a sloth move?
A) Quickly
B) Slowly
C) Angrily
D) Backwards
Answer: B

2. What special design do zebras have on their fur?
A) Stripes
B) Spots
C) Zigzags
D) Plaid
Answer: A

3. Where do elephants live?
A) In South America
B) In the Arctic
C) In Africa and Asia
D) Underwater
Answer: C

4. Groups of animals have different names. What is a group of lions called?
A) A gang
B) A pride
C) A club
D) Scary
Answer: B

5. What is a narwhal's tusk good for?
A) Making shish kebabs
B) Roasting marshmallows
C) Nothing
D) Jousting
Answer: D

A Narwhal Song

On Top of a Narwhal
(to the tune of "On Top of Old Smokey")

On top of a narwhal,
So pointy and strong,
There is a hard tusk
That can be ten feet long.

The tusk is for jousting,
Just like a sword fight,
A narwhal will tap it
With all of his might.

Sometimes narwhal tusks will
Wash up on the shore,
And people once sold them,
As unicorn horns!

Note: For a metric version of this song, insert "That's three meters long"
as the last line in the first chorus.

Polar Match-Up

Materials:
Matching Cards (pp. 51-52), crayons or markers, scissors, envelopes (one per child)

Preparation:
Duplicate a copy of the Matching Cards for each child.

Directions:
1. Give each child a set of the Matching Cards to color and cut apart. The children can store the cards in the envelopes.
2. Have the children take the card game home to play with their families. If the children can't read the facts, the adults can help.

Option:
• Have the children make their own match-up games.

Did You Know...
A polar bear has fur between its toes to keep it from slipping or sliding on the ice!

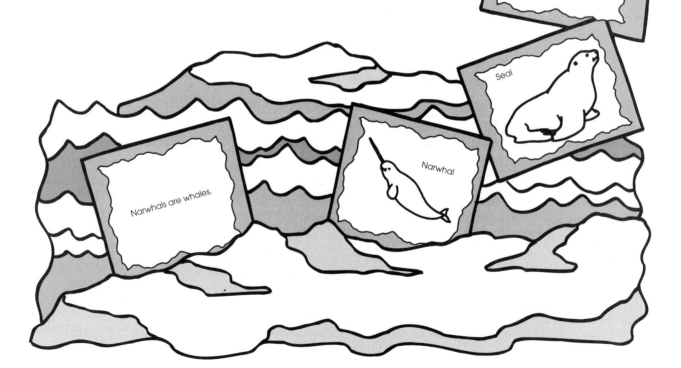

A Is for Animals © 2001 Monday Morning Books

Matching Cards

Polar Bear

Seal

Arctic Fox

Penguin

Arctic Hare

Narwhal

Matching Cards

Penguins have webbed feet and paddle-like flippers.

Polar bears eat fish and seals.

Arctic foxes have pure white fur in the winter and gray fur in the summer.

Seals have been hunted for their furs.

Arctic hares are camouflaged by their white fur.

Narwhals are whales.

If You Give a Bear a Bagel

This activity takes a well-known children's book and lets the children rewrite it featuring animals that live in forests or in the mountains.

Materials:
If You Give a Mouse a Cookie, *If You Give a Moose a Muffin*, or *If You Give a Pig a Pancake*, all by Laura Joffe Numeroff, paper, pens or pencils, crayons and markers, chalk, chalkboard, books about animals in the forest and mountains

Preparation:
Write a list of forest and mountain animals on the chalkboard (see below).

Directions:
1. Read one of the *If You Give...* books to the children.
2. Explain that the children will be writing their own short stories featuring an animal that lives in the forest or mountains.
3. The children can choose animals from the list on the chalkboard, or they can look through forest and mountain resources to find their own.
4. Have the children write short stories about their animals.
5. The children can illustrate the stories when they're finished.

Options:
• The children can add facts about their featured animals.
• The children can share their stories with other classes.

Forest and Mountain Animals:
Alpaca, bear, bighorn sheep, bobcat, deer, elk, fox, hawk, llama, moose, mountain goat, owl, panda, rabbit, snow leopard, yak

Bamboo Math

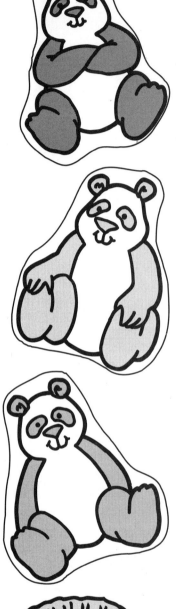

Materials:
Pandas, craft sticks, glue, paper plates, scissors, crayons or markers

Preparation:
Duplicate enough of the panda patterns for each child to have one.

Directions:
1. Explain that the children will each be making a three-dimensional math problem.
2. Demonstrate the activity. Glue a panda to a paper plate. Then add craft sticks to the left and right of the panda. Finally, write in a +, -, or x sign on the panda's belly. The problem will be the number of craft sticks on the left plus, minus, or times the number of craft sticks on the right. Write the answer on the back of the plate.
3. Let the children create their own problems and write the answers on the back.
4. Check them to make sure the answers are correct. Then let the children switch problems with each other.

Did You Know...
Pandas live in China and eat bamboo.

A Is for Animals © 2001 Monday Morning Books

Pandas

Hooray for Hibernating

Certain animals, such as bears, spend the winter hibernating in an inactive (sleep-like) state.

Materials:
Paper, crayons or markers, scissors

Preparation:
Cut the papers to look like the type of "do not disturb" signs that hang on a hotel door.

Directions:
1. Explain the concept of hibernating to the children.
2. Tell the children that they will be making signs for their bedroom doors to let people know when they will be in an inactive state (sleeping).
3. Have the children draw a picture of a bear sleeping. They should write "Do Not Disturb—Hibernating" on the sign.

Option:
• Provide resources about hibernating for the children to look through. They can choose to draw specific animals from the books.

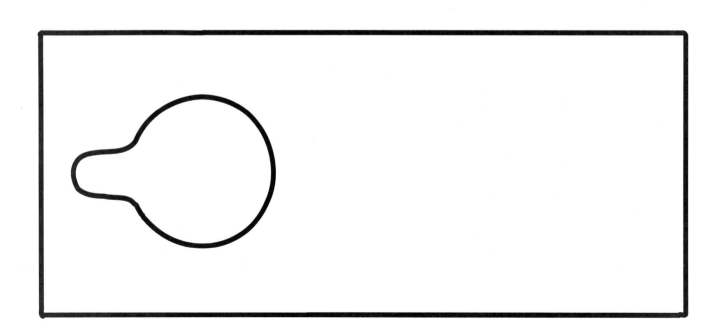

A Is for Animals © 2001 Monday Morning Books

Mountain of Words

This spelling activity features a bulletin board decorated to look like a mountain. The spelling words are written on animals that live in the mountains.

Materials:
Mountain Animals (p. 58), bag, construction paper (brown, white, green), scissors, colored markers, tape

Preparation:
1. Duplicate a copy of the Mountain Animals for each child and one for teacher use.
2. Cut the animals apart and color as desired.
3. Create a mountain background using the construction paper.

Directions:
1. Announce a date for a spelling bee.
2. Divide the students into small groups. Have the children work together to learn the words. Let the children take the words home to study.
3. On the day of the spelling bee, put the animals in a bag. Pull one animal from the bag at a time and have a child from each group spell the word on the animal.
4. If the child spells the word correctly, he or she can post the animal on the board. If not, another child from that group tries to spell the word.
5. Continue until each child has a chance to spell one word and all of the animals are posted on the board.

Option:
• If the words are too difficult, white-out the given spelling words and write in your own. Duplicate these for the class.

Mountain Animals

Panda Bear

Vicuña

Llama

Yak

Bobcat

Snow Leopard

Mountain Goat

Beautiful Snow Leopard

Snow leopards are found in the mountains of central Asia. They are large, whitish cats and can have many dark blotches on their fur.

Materials:
Butcher paper, tempera paint, paintbrushes, shallow tins (for paint)

Preparation:
None

Directions:
1. Describe snow leopards to the children. If possible, show them a picture of a snow leopard from a photography book.
2. Explain that the children will be working as a class to make a large snow leopard.
3. Draw an outline of the snow leopard on a large sheet of butcher paper. Use the picture on this page as an example.
4. Let the children work in teams to paint the snow leopard.
5. Once the poster dries, save it for the "Spotting a Snow Leopard" activity (p. 60).

Options:
• Let the children use fabric (such as fun fur) to cover the snow leopard.
• Have the children make miniature snow leopards.

Spotting a Snow Leopard

This game uses the poster-sized snow leopard that the children made in this week's featured art activity.

Materials:
Snow Leopard (p. 59), black self-sticking dots, blindfold (optional)

Preparation:
None

Directions:
1. Describe snow leopards to the children.
2. Place the snow leopard at an appropriate level on a wall.
3. Explain to the children that they will be playing a game similar to "Pin the tail on the donkey."
4. Give the first child one self-sticking dot, and either blindfold the child or have the child close his or her eyes.
5. Have the children attempt to pin the spot on the snow leopard.
6. Make sure each child has a chance to play the game.

Did You Know...
Unlike a house cat that purrs when it's happy, a snow leopard's purr means "watch out!"

A Is for Animals © 2001 Monday Morning Books

Forest Song

Take Me Out to the Forest
(to the tune of "Take Me Out to the Ball Game")

Take me out to the forest,
Take me up in the hills,
I want to visit the pandas there,
Even though I know that they aren't bears.

Oh, a panda eats lots of bamboo.
It munches and munches all day.
And I want to go to China
Where the pandas play.

Animal Concentration

Materials:
Mountain Animals (p. 58), paper, crayons or markers, cardstock, scissors, envelopes (one per child)

Preparation:
Duplicate two copies of the Mountain Animals for each child.

Directions:
1. Give each child two copies of the patterns to color and cut out.
2. Have the children cut the cardstock into squares. They should glue one pattern onto each square.
3. Teach the children the concentration game. They turn all of the cards face-down. Then they take turns flipping two cards over. If the pictures on the cards match, they keep both and try again. If the cards don't match, they turn them face-down and another child takes a turn.
4. The children can take the concentration game home in the envelopes to play with their families.

Option:
• Older children can practice spelling the names of the animals as they turn over the cards.

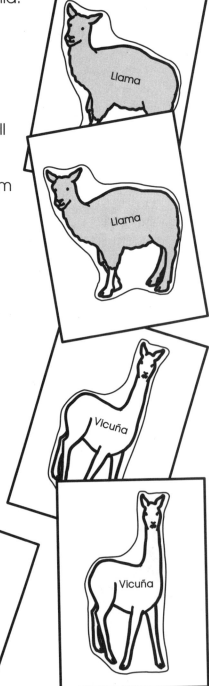

A Is for Animals © 2001 Monday Morning Books

Animal Book Links

Big Cats by Seymour Simon (HarperCollins, 1992).

Great Ice Bear by Dorothy Hinshaw Patent (Morrow, 1999).
Beautiful illustrations accompany a rich text. Choose facts to share.

Harp Seal Pups by Downs Matthews (Simon & Schuster, 1997).
Children are sure to be charmed by the photographs of adorable baby seals!

The Leopard Family Book by Jonathan Scott (Picture Book Studio, 1991).
Sleek leopards in their natural habitats grace the pages of this resource.

Llama by Caroline Arnold (Morrow, 1988).
This author also wrote *Camel, Giraffe, Kangaroo, Koala, Penguin,* and *Zebra*.

Mind-Blowing Mammals by Leslie Elliott (Sterling, 1994).

The Polar Bear on the Ice by Martin Banks (Gareth Stevens, 1989).
This book includes an interesting food chain to share.

Polar Bears by Lesley A. DuTemple (Lerner, 1997).
This book includes chapters on seal hunting and swimming in ice water.

Safari by Caren Barzelay Stelson (Carolrhoda, 1988).
Amazing photographs of lions, hyenas, lizards, zebras, wildebeasts and other animals of Africa fill this book.

The Sea World Book of Penguins by Frank S. Todd (Harcourt Brace Jovanovich, 1981).
This book includes incredible photos.

Tiger, Tiger Growing Up... by Joan Hewett (Clarion, 1993).

To the Top of the World: Adventures with Arctic Wolves by Jim Brandenburg (Walker, 1993).
There are beautiful pictures to share.

The World of Penguins by David Saintsing (Gareth Stevens, 1988).
The enemies and defense chapter is extremely interesting.

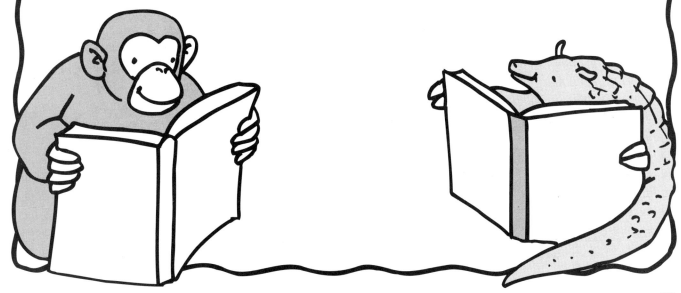

Name

HAS MASTERED

THE WORLD OF

ANIMALS

AND IS AN HONORARY ZOOLOGIST.

HONORARY ZOOLOGIST